Love

& Other Things

Love

& Other Things

The poems and letters written during the many
stages of love, from the first meeting,
to the inevitable end

PHILIP GIBBONS

BREWIN BOOKS

Love can make you emotionally strong, as well as emotionally insecure, at various stages during a relationship.

However, love should give you the courage to be honest with the one you love, and the one that you once loved.

HAVE YOU THE COURAGE?

First published by
Brewin Books Ltd, 56 Alcester Road,
Studley, Warwickshire B80 7LG in 2010
www.brewinbooks.com

ISBN: 978-1-85858-469-0

A Cataloguing in Publication Record
for this title is available from the British Library.

Typeset in Sabon
Printed in Great Britain by
Hobbs the Printers Ltd.

Contents

The Many Stages of Love   9

1)   The Beginning   11
2)   The Romance   12
3)   The Dream   16
4)   The Commitment   17
5)   The Innocence   18
6)   Always and Forever   19
7)   The Happiness   20
8)   The Tolerance   22
9)   The Insecurity   24
10)   The Awkward Stage   26
11)   The Need   29
12)   The Pleading   33
13)   The Hurt   34
14)   The Tragedy   40
15)   The Reality   44
16)   The End   51

Other Things   55

Letters   66

Part 1:   Letters from 'G'   67
Part 2:   Letters from 'J'   83
Part 3:   Letters from 'D'   91
Part 4:   Letters from 'M'   95

The following poems are the
opinions of one, so the 'victims'
are unable to reply.

They probably have their
own version of events, but on
ex-lovers, you cannot rely.

1.

The Beginning

Any Regrets?

You must believe that words written by lovers, are meant from deep within their heart. However, time goes by, then lovers part. Perhaps they marry and live their lives. Much later, they may feel moments of nostalgia, as they remember the days of a previous love. But those days are gone, so they live on distant memories, cleansed by the passing years.

Those memories could have been reality!

Love Grows

Don't be a fool, don't let it go.
It may only come once, just let it grow.

Fall

If she's the one, accept it.
Don't fight it, respect it.

I Know

You don't know what love is, until it hits you.
And when it hits you, you don't get up.

2.

The Romance

Free Love

I hope you are aware, that I'm not a Registered Charity.
But as I adore you with all my heart, my love for you is free.

In Praise Of Older Women

She would be nearly seventy now, and forty when we met.
But don't think for one minute, her love I will forget.

Elusive Butterflies

Thinking of me made her giddy, she said, it gave her, butterflies.
So how could I love another, when for her my heart still cries.

Answer Me

Can I ask you a question please, maybe two or three.
Don't tell me face to face, just send them back to me.
   1) Do you think you will love me forever?
   2) Will you love someone else, one day?
   3) Do I make you happy?

I Hope So

She read my letter at the bus stop, going home that night.
She said she felt so close to me, and fall in love, we might.

A Decent Proposal

You seem far more attractive as a spinster, than someone's doting wife.
But I'll still go ahead and marry you, but it will only be for life.

Glasses

The girl with the glasses, on the end of her nose,
I'd like to be with her, wherever she goes.
I've fallen for her, I'm certain she knows.
That girl with the glasses, on the end of her nose.

The Unwitting Testimony

"Thank you for being the best Christmas present I ever had".
Her sweet card had stated.
To receive that from her, meant that she loved me. Backdated!

'And'

She didn't much care, when she started a sentence with 'And'.
Those letters were special. Lovers I know, understand.

Her First Letter

She had been wondering lately, if I wouldn't mind a chat.
A chat about nothing really, only this and that.
She would like once more to see me, if not, she'd understand.
She then became my greatest love, who says your life's not planned?

Love Has No Boundaries

I wish you didn't love me, I can't think why you do?
I really am such a horrible, insecure, mixed up, immature, snivelling,
feeling sorry for myself, kind of person, but I always will love you.

In Praise Of Car Parks

Snatched moments of happiness, to play out loves theme.
It's as if harsh reality, would spoil our heart's dream.

Heartburn

It's only because I loved her, that occasionally I'd let,
her sit down with her thoughts, and enjoy a cigarette.

Sweet Melody

When you are in love, always believe in the words of a song.
They were written for you, and love can't be wrong.

Still

Enormous cards, in a box,
Her pretty face, those summer frocks
That special look, those auburn locks,
I love her still, turn back the clocks.

Internal Memo

She wrote me on office memo paper,
Addressed it to P.G.
I thought it a sweet and lovely gesture,
How romantic can you be?

Last Post

She would often post a love letter, at midnight in the rain.
It made her feel romantic, how I wish for one again.

Will You?

She always thought that our love was special,
affection, never lust.
She often felt shy and unsure.
Marry that girl? Yes, I must.

My Friend

Who did she want? No one but me.
How could I not love her. My sweet girl, Ami.

3.

The Dream

Lovers Only

I hardly want to marry you, or even change your life.
It would be nice to be with you, but I'm not looking for a wife.
If there's any kind of hope for us, I'll put you on the list.
Of those I feel I could have loved, and happy that I kissed.

Reminiscing

I often read her letters, it can take up all the day.
It makes me feel so close to her, as if she's never been away.

She Asked

Can we please go and watch the boats, and things again.
Like we did that Saturday morning, when all it did was rain.
When all this is over and done with, and my heart's not dulled with pain.
Please let us re-live that special day, when life was oh! so plain.

Wishing

All those wonderful letters, then she went away.
If only I could receive one, preferably today.

Oh! Henry

I wish you a wonderful wife and children, with a life full of this and that.
That you deserve, but all I can provide, is Henry, my lovable cat.

The Commitment

Warning

When you fall in love with me, you put your heart upon the line.
It usually ends in tears, but I'm not ashamed to say, they're mine.

I Saved Her

I saved myself – but nobody waits anymore.
I saved myself – what did I save myself for.
I saved myself – never done anything like this before.

The Girl Can't Help It

I would hardly describe her, as a dull Philistine.
But as a friend and a lover, she's perfectly fine.

First Class

She went along with her mother, to midnight mass.
She told God she loved me, oh! That girl had class.

Worthy

She mentioned that I was the nicest man she had known,
not including her dad.
Thinking about it later, that was the nicest compliment I've had.

5.

The Innocence

Never Forgotten

So I kept her photograph, as memories are great.
We hardly kissed or anything, that sweet girl in Margate.

You Jane, Me Sent

That pretty blonde girl, whose mother served tea.
I won't mention her name, let's call her Jane P.
We went out for a while, Blondie and me.
Her mother found out, hello! Coventry.

Her Attempt At Emotional Blackmail

I'm just taking my temperature, not as if you care,
It should be 96, but it's 98, so there!!

Name Names

She was named after that beauty in 'Gone with the Wind'.
No wonder with my heart, my greatest love is twinned.

Can't Hurry Love

Why not like me a little? But don't fall for me.
There's no need to hurry, it will come naturally.

6.

Always And Forever

Today I Promise

If you believed all those lovers, who promised to love you for always and forever, and to remain with you for evermore. Then none of us would get past the first hurdle of life.

As we know, love can be fickle, and those words of love are only meant for that moment in time, as we cannot possibly know how we will feel tomorrow. But our hearts cannot stop making those promises.

A Romantic Sick Note

I think about you quite often, especially since I've been ill.
I need you. I think that's what it is. I love you and always will.

Sing It To Me

I love you so much, my wonderful man.
Who never bothers to ring, or perhaps give a damn.
But I just can't help it, I hopelessly am.
In love with my sweetheart, as only I can.

Beyond Belief

Her words of 'Love Forever', I don't believe them as a rule.
But for a while I dropped my guard, and believed her like a fool.

The Happiness

It's Her

Throughout the years, I could always rely,
On that wonderful girl, a little too shy.
No questions asked, not one to pry,
I care for her deeply, now you know why.

Perfect

You had hardly any imperfections, when I first met you.
But I love you even more today, now that you have a few.

Love Her Still

I held her, loved her, in her prime.
She totally loved me, a love sublime.
She's aged a little, but that's no crime.
I only wish, that I could turn back time.

Don't Ever Change

Sometimes I stop and glance at her.
Would I occasionally, a pretty girl prefer?
But imperfections are attractive too.
That's what I love, when I look at you.

Nature Will Wait

Look here you! I'm spending too much time on river banks.
Would you mind if tomorrow, we can do some shopping? Thanks.

Kiss And Make Up

"Have you decided that without make-up, I'm not that particularly nice?"

Reply:

"No sweetheart. I think you're beautiful.
In my heart, you will always suffice."

Is This A Compliment?

She thought we were meant for each other.
Then she explained just why.
I'd been such a toad, so she had been sent.
To teach me a lesson, to tease and torment.
As a gift from the great one on high.
(With apologies to all toads).

My My

Give me a girl myopic, with glasses any day.
She sees the world through a mist, and looks at me that way.

8.

The Tolerance

It Will Pass

Your beauty hangs, but by a thread,
The passing time, I know you dread.
The twilight years, you have yet to tread,
There are some thoughts, best left unsaid.

Shame Faced

A pretty face, just my kind.
If only she had a pretty mind.

Well, Have You?

Have you fallen in love with another yet?
Are you seeing someone, you have recently met?
If you find someone else, I really won't mind,
But don't fall in love, just be perfectly kind.

Intolerable

Her valentine cards, were a little too much.
I was never more than, her emotional crutch.
We had little in common, no love life as such.
Whatever we had, we are no longer in touch.

Thank You

If you had never decided, to finish with me.
Then how would I have met, those lovers to be.

To You

You saw my kindness as a weakness, that I won't repeat.
Another chance will not arrive, for you to so mistreat.

Sometimes (1)

Sometimes – the breeze, it can get you.
Sometimes – you'd fall, if I let you.
Sometimes – I'd rather forget you.
Sometimes.

Users

She was looking for someone to love her, so decided I would do.
So she chased me until she got me, she certainly did pursue.
Then along came someone else, before I even knew.
But if I was being honest, I felt I used her too.

A Normal Day At The Office

I know we used to fight and argue, but you were the highlight of my day.
I so miss that and think of you, keep in touch, OK!

Can't Move On

Perhaps the reason why you hunger, for those you loved before,
Is because you've reached that stage, you don't go looking anymore.

9.

The Insecurity

Lover Come Back

I altered this year's diary, with just one nagging doubt.
I'll give you maybe one more year, and then I'll leave you out.

Easily Fooled

I'm a poor judge of character, my perception is not up to much.
But as far as falling in love is concerned, I'm just an easy touch.

Beware

Give a girl her own space and she will disappear into it.

Deluded

No calls returned, so I assume she's gone.
But there's a queue for me, of maybe one.
At the moment, it's a little slow.
But just you watch it, grow and grow.

A Willing Victim

I don't mind being used in the least.
But not emotionally!

It's Shorter Than You Think

I would like to fall in love with you, before it gets too late.
It soon won't really matter, if we continue just to wait.
But time is running over, so let's wipe clean the slate.
Too much talking, let's move on, and leave the long debate.

Words Of Love

The more they say 'I love you', I would question their intent.
It's their insecurity that needs you, perhaps those words aren't meant?

The Trouble With Love Letters

Your heart is telling you what to write, rather than your mind.
But my mind reads what your heart is saying, no wonder love is blind.

Don't Ask

You shouldn't make decisions about love,
when you are emotionally unstable.
I'm hardly capable of making decisions about love,
when I'm willing and able.

10.
The Awkward Stage

Perfectionist

It's hardly now that I'm concerned about, she's been a perfect joy.
I'm a little worried in the future, that her habits might annoy.

It's Not Big, See

There she was in her car, smoking, honestly.
Does she think I'm going to fall for her, just to lose her to Big C.

Martyr

How could I ever say goodbye, to a girl once loved,
who would ask me why?
I would rather her say farewell to me, then suffer myself her misery.

More Second Thoughts

Am I quite ready for the Tesco queue?
For that's my future, if I stay with you.
But life's too short and opportunities few.
An excellent decision from my point of view.

Grow Up

I thought her a little special, but that was not her fault.
You should be more responsible, when you become adult.

As If!

As you no longer seem to want me, can I take out your best friend.
I thought I'd mention it to you, as I would rather not offend.
The two of us together, means the less time you will spend.
With me, with her, with both of us, it's what was needed in the end.

Get Out Clause

Will she turn into her mother? I suppose there's half a chance,
I'd better call an end to things, and make this our last dance.

Invisible Ink

Expensive cards, but her words were cheap,
Hollow meanings and not too deep.

An Only Child

As a single child of a loving pair,
She doesn't feel the need to share.
Of others needs, she is unaware,
Perhaps that explains, her lack of care.

No Future

I found her quite appealing, if the truth was said.
If only she didn't smoke, or fancy garlic bread.

Love Or Nothing At All

You know, it's just the way it is with me.
It can never be friendship, after love, you see.

Great Pretender

Are you aware, that the meaning of forever, is for all time, without end?
So why did you say you would love me forever, or perhaps, it was only pretend.

Let Down Gently

She apologised for ignoring me, as our friendship meant so much.
But when she's pulled herself together, she promised to get in touch.

How, Why And When?

Nothing in common, slowly drifting apart.
How in the first place, did love ever start?

Wrong Choice

Her perception of me, is not what I see.
Must get out of there fast, this love, cannot last.

Meaningless

Your never ending words of love, were lacking honesty.
I for one, saw through those words, I knew the truth you see.

The Need

You! You! You!

You probably feel, that this is all about me.
But I'd just like to tell you, in all honesty.
I'm a 'bit part' player, this is all about you.
You made me love you, but you never knew.

A Cry From The Heart

To be perfectly honest, I don't wish you well.
I am the heart, that you failed to tell.
I was that love, with whom you once fell.
Now you know why, I don't wish you well.

Be More Choosy

She spoke of herself, time and again.
Her expectations of me, were certainly plain.
I found all her needs, an emotional drain.
As I felt that her love, would be hard to maintain.

I Wonder

My memories of, another time and place.
When you were young, with a pretty face.
Of the broken heart, there is little trace.
But what might have been, do my thoughts embrace.

Don't Try To Understand

She rang me and pursued me, hardly leaving me alone.
When I said I'd see her, she told me not to phone.

How Could I?

She hoped I would meet someone, then live, happily.
But said, please don't love her, as you have loved me.

Late Payer

You may have been there, in her time of need,
But that, she would rather forget.
She didn't much care when the roles were reversed,
She owes, an emotional debt.

Cue Love

For you my love, I joined the queue.
It's not a thing, I would usually do.
To whom I write, can't tell you who.
But how I wish, you only knew.

Avoiding Heartbreak

You love her and you want her, but it doesn't go to plan.
You need to move on, honestly! As quickly as you can.

7pm – Saturday

Tea on the table, like military precision.
Never quite able, to make a decision.
Her washing-up done, as if on a mission.
Where was the love? For me, no admission.

Heartbreaker

Romance is so superficial, according to the smart.
Just they try telling that, to my broken heart.

Simplicity

She left so quietly, not even a row.
But to be perfectly honest, I'm missing her now.

Miss You Too

Selfish thoughts, they do exist.
You hate yourself, but can't resist.
The one desire, that those you kissed.
Regret the love, they surely missed.

Kiss Goodbye

I seldom think about her now,
In fact it's her I hardly miss.
What I long for, are those lips.
She just knew how to kiss.

What Will Become?

Occasionally, you need a broken heart,
To urge you on to greater things.
Let's not expect too much, too soon,
Just see what the future brings.

Your Day Will Come

You know she won't return.
But still, her love, you yearn.
One day, you'll surely learn.
That perhaps, it's not your turn.

Never Goodbye

It's now the beginning of two thousand and ten.
So I thought I would read your letters again.
It's twenty years plus, since they were written.
Do you know that today, I still remain smitten.

Still Waiting

If our last words were 'I love you',
How come I've yet to hear.
That you miss and need me badly,
Or have even shed a tear.

12.

The Pleading

Losing Your Religion

To run off like a feeblite, was that the thing to do?
Did 'believing' really teach you this, or if not, tell me who?

Desperate Man

In desperation when she left, I said, 'Will you marry me'?
I'm now so grateful to that girl, that she ignored my plea.

I Will

I'll get through all this, no matter how.
That's if my heart, will only allow.

Thought

I thought I only wanted you,
But now, I know I need you.

Fickle

I do not accept your criticism, you feel you have to bring.
While your praise is always welcome, but that's another thing.

Nothing Said

Your unwritten words, said so much to me.
No goodbye, no farewell, and no apology.

13.

The Hurt

Knowing Fools

We fool ourselves occasionally, it's maybe what we need.
Better that, than to accept the truth, then our wounded hearts would bleed.

Don't Give In

Following months of all this heartbreak stuff.
You would have thought by now, I would have had enough.
While my heart was treated, a little rough.
You must hang on in there, when the going gets tough.

Different Viewpoints

It was hardly a serious love affair, from her personal point of view.
But to me, it seemed so special, with that stranger I hardly knew.

Double Fault

It's not the love that is lost, that's part of the game.
It's her lack of respect, that hurts, she's to blame.

Overspent

Those words I wish you truly meant,
I couldn't read them, our love was spent.

Sweet

Strong and silent is all very well, but it's your broken heart she took.
But revenge is far more sweeter, rather than let her off the hook.

Yes! You Should

Your apology is unacceptable, it is hardly worth debate.
You should have thought more at the time, you should have told me straight.

Found Out

I'm awfully glad you found someone else, before dispensing with me.
I would have hated the thought of loving one, so lacking and weak, morally.

Leave Her Wanting

She doesn't want you, she left you flat.
There's something else, even more than that.
She just couldn't like you, any less.
But would hate it if, you found happiness.

Schadenfreude

The thought of me unhappy, would make you overjoyed.
It would give you a little more time, to practice Schadenfreude.

Is Silence Golden?

I would rather not forgive you, I prefer to let it lie.
In time to come, you may feel the need, to speak and tell me why?

Selected Memory

How cruel she thought, when he left, to treat her so unfair.
He had thought of leaving many times, while she was unaware.
She once treated someone else like that, just left, without a care.
Will she be feeling sorry for herself? I'm sure, she wouldn't dare.

Too Starry-Eyed

That love affair, you thought all too brief.
Ecstatic feelings, then disbelief.
So it then all ends, in hurtful grief.
Why steal your love? Like a heartless thief.

Please Tell

You know, I've thought about this at length,
You say your belief, gives you an inner strength.
So why do you then, refuse to face?
Those who once, you did embrace.

Cruel Fool

Don't be cruel to a heart that's true,
Did the great man sing, but then, he knew.
That you respect a love, as it grew.
If he knew that, why didn't you?

In Too Deep

Please don't ever weaken and say 'let's start again'.
I'd rather just dislike you and let the hurt remain.

Sincerity

I am so pleased to hear, that you have 'found your feet'.
It's just a great pity, that you never found your heart.

Lost In The Post

In desperation I wrote, 'We will always belong'.
She didn't reply, this fool was wrong.

Seeing Is Believing

How long will it take, for you to see, the error of your ways?
I only hope I don't meet you next, when you've seen much better days.

Time Will Tell

Love letters are timeless, may their message never fade.
Unless sent by a careless heart, who once, your love betrayed.

Careless

If you found the strength, for my heart to tear.
Surely you could find, the strength to care.

Shortsighted

You fell for me, I liked your mind.
The sort of girl I thought, 'she's kind'.
A little myopic, but I didn't mind.
For love's like you, a little blind.

Broken

From a love, that grew and grew.
To a stranger, you hardly knew.

Fragile Heart

Yesterday's love, could not hear the cries.
From a heart she left wanting, still broken, it lies.
To love far too deeply, is a little unwise.
When the price that you pay, is hurt, when love dies.

Only Reluctantly

That's my trouble, I refuse to plead.
For a love now gone and a heart in need.
A cruel and selfish act indeed.
On my broken heart, did her ego feed.

It Matters

Does any of this really matter, if so, tell me how?
Time will heal a broken heart, so it surely matters now.

Who Are You?

There will be a time, when we may meet.
We will walk on by, we will not greet.
Your words of love, now obsolete.
Yet used by you, to so mistreat.

Never

You made someone happy, it certainly wasn't me.
I never felt that special love, I hoped would always be.

Feeblite

So you've gone and found another, as you cannot do what's right.
You should have told him a while ago, you selfish feeblite.

Hard Lines

Dividing lines, not parallel.
In between, in love you fell.
Were you sure? You couldn't tell.
But then you thought, you knew her well.

The Tragedy

Hypocrite!

I hope your man is not as cruel, when he allocates your place.
In his world of many mansions, it will be him, you'll have to face.

That Love

That love, you thought so special.
That love, you once embraced.
That love, you thought forever.
That love, was such as waste.

The Christmas Card

That cold unwelcome, at your door,
That saddened soul, you loved no more.
Why be cruel? When the heart is raw,
To that broken hearted fool, you saw.

Don't Go Back!

She wouldn't even face you, so she couldn't see the pain.
Is this the kind of person, that you could ever love again?

Blind Alley

I'd rather not forgive you, if you honestly don't mind.
I'm just a little sensitive, as to why, love is so blind.

Never Expect More

Why do we expect a little more,
From those we loved, from a time before.
You see them through, love lost eyes,
The truth is brutal, when love dies.

Oh! Really

It's not just you, who's made a fool of me.
It's love, it's life, it's reality.

Only One Winner

I always felt that religion was her crutch, but no!
I was her crutch. Religion was her iron rod.
So I was in a no-win situation. You can't compete against her God.

You Can't Fool Me

You're not street-wise, you're just laid back.
You live your life, in a cul-de-sac.
Your sun-kissed days, they will not last.
Unlike the myths, grown out of memories past.

Aftermath

The end of love may bring, some selfish words that sting.
With such a hollow ring, like leeches, how they cling.

How?

I fell in love with who she used to be, not the girl, that she became.
How can you lose your greatest love? Then dislike her, all the same.

Grounded

She asked me to leave you, but I never would.
So I burnt all my bridges, I felt that I could.
No chance to return, emotions adrift.
The end and the heartbreak, arrived, oh so swift.

Final Goodbye

She sent her final birthday card, addressed to 'Special Friend'.
These words were her last to me, before she reached the end.
"This may be your last special birthday card from me,
So enjoy today, for the two of us".

Be Yourself

While we need revenge so sweet.
Not too harshly, shall we treat.
Those who hurt us, or our downfall greet.
We can't be like them, they lie and cheat.

'Always' – At All Times

It seems, a great deal of your time was spent,
In writing those special words you sent.
You mentioned 'always', so how was it, you went?
Are you quite sure, you knew what it meant.

An Apology?

She said that she still loved me, but felt it was too late.
Then maybe not on second thoughts, our love was always great.
Oh why? She then continued, did we ever split.
My fault, my love insisted, I dislike myself for it.

Indecent Proposal

Many times she would ask, "Will you marry me?"
I could never say 'I will', but I may eventually.
Then when she left I wrote to her, "Will you marry me?"
But no reply, or any call, life's just so cruel you see.

Welcome Overstayed

I felt I never knew, the stranger she became.
So I stayed a while longer, but she never seemed the same.
There were never lover's questions, so I have myself to blame.
I was unprepared for the end, when suddenly it came.

15.

The Reality

Nobody's Fool

The fool who fails to read the signs.
Is blinded by the love he pines.
As love when gone, so slow declines.
Is he a fool, that true love binds?

That's Heartbreak

Over your life, you probably spend a year, with a broken heart.
But on reflection, it's worth it, of life, it's just a small part.

Beware!

What you may feel is cruel and wild.
Comes naturally, to an only child.

Outdated

If you're reading this, then it's far too late.
Our love is well past, it's sell-by-date.
There was a time, when I thought I'd wait.
But you never came, then that's our fate.

No Entry

Grim reality, keep away.
We know you're out there,
That's where you'll stay.

Pay Attention

You allowed it all to happen, you watched and let it slip.
You saw the heartache coming and you failed to take a grip.

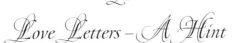

Love Letters – A Hint

Perhaps you are using 'always' and 'forever' too freely.
It's probably best to use them, when you mean them, sincerely.

Final Comment

Will I see her again? Hopefully not.
I would like to avoid her, no matter what.
Although our affair, was not worth a lot.
So let's leave it there, as one we forgot.

Another Lesson

If you've asked for her hand and she fails to reply.
Get out of there, this means goodbye.

Can You?

Yes, we know you're hurting, but never let them see.
Let them live their selfish lives, so hide your misery.
Don't wait for explanations, you're bound to disagree.
Why waste your time on careless hearts, why not just let it be.

Cat Flap

After a while, I did realise.
She had little about her, a dull second prize.
Who would have thought, she would be one to despise.
I was blinded by love and those 'pussycat eyes'.

Who Needs You?

Can you once again confirm, you have said your last farewell.
As there are one or two others interested, it's going rather well.

Mirror, Mirror

You feel on reflection, that you knew all along.
That you and her love, just didn't belong.
You had little in common, but sang the same song.
So take a look at yourself, you were hopelessly wrong.

Advantage Love

Advantage, yes she took.
But you let her off the hook.
As you played it by the book.
Perhaps next time, you'll look.

Phoney

The age of the love letter, seems long gone and flown.
It's got so much to answer for, that mobile phone.

Well Rid

If she's gone, then let her go.
Don't plead with her, don't stoop so low.
You'd hate yourself, at least you know.
Her worthless love, would never grow.

Accepted

That pretty girl, I thought so sweet.
She once adored me, then found her feet.
With her selfish heart, I can't compete.
So accept the truth and admit defeat.

Pretence

Her words were not her feelings, but what she thought I'd like to hear.
Was it really worth the effort, to fall for one so insincere.

Was It Love?

Is the heartbreak coming? If so, bring it on.
But when I thought of her just now, I'm almost pleased she's gone.

Come On Up

Don't complain, when it arrives.
It's called come-uppance, on fools it thrives.

The Stages Of Love (Abridged Version)

1) The beginning.
2) The end of the beginning.
3) The beginning of the end.
4) The end.

I Paid The Price

Her Valentine Card had said, 'You are definitely the one'.
She paid four pounds eighty nine for it. The price, she left it on.
It had cost an awful lot of money, then suddenly we lost touch.
But at the time, she thought me worth it, now it's not worth half as much.

A Friend Indeed

So you've gone off with another then.
Thanks for telling him, why and when.
Do you honestly feel, he deserved this end.
I expected more from you, my former friend.

Falling

I suppose we had little in common, emotionally nothing at all.
It seems to take years, to see the plain truth, then ask yourself, why did I fall?

Almost

She settled for home comforts, it was creeping up on me.
To see her every day, I didn't notice change you see.
She'd wake up in the morning, then switch on her T.V.
It's a blessing that she left me, of her small world, I'm free.

Sometimes (2)

Sometimes – The slightest of glances.
Sometimes – Can bring sweet romances.
Sometimes – They can spoil all your chances.
Sometimes.

Only One

Just one lifetime – that's all you get.
Don't spend your days, in deep regret.

Science

I had hoped to fall in love with you, but there's no chemistry in between.
You're just the kind of girl I like, isn't life just mean?

High Time

I feel I've given you far too much, of my important time.
I have a book to write , poems to recite, and mountains yet to climb.

Time Heals

Revenge from me was never planned,
As fate gave me a helping hand.
I've seen her life, it's not too grand.
Her looks have faded, I understand.

The Right Way

So blunt, as well as dignified.
She bid farewell, I hardly cried.
I respected her, she hadn't lied.
She was unlike you, so lacking pride.

Chasing Rainbows

So you think you're on a journey, where you will find your rainbow's end.
The rainbow's end is here and now, not in the prayers you send.

Careless Hands

I'm now so very well aware, she's washed her hands of me.
But what I can't quite understand, is that, she never washed her hands for tea.

It's Not You

Her pretence to be romantic, her letters seemed for real.
When I look back at those words, it's just a fool I feel.

I Sent Them Back

From a 'I will love you, forever', to a 'Someone Special' card.
I'm afraid I'll have to tell her, it shouldn't be too hard.
I don't need your hollow words, please take them. Have them back.
It's honesty and sincerity, I'm certain that they lack.

Be Gentle

To treat him cold and harshly, you may well feel inclined.
But it can be just as easy, to be a little kind.

Is That It Then?

I suppose I was surprised, as I thought it, just a phase.
When she announced, that our love, had seen much better days.
But if that is what she wanted, I would willingly erase.
All the love, we both once shared, then go our separate ways.

Don't Count On It

You seem almost far too sure, of your Heavenly place.
Don't take it for granted, perhaps not, in your case.
All your selfish thoughts, with a certain lack of grace.
You will hardly fool him, when you come face to face.

16.

The End

Has-Been

You've said it so often, it's now all been said.
No sweet words to write, those words have been read.
No romance to share, all the hurt that you dread.
It's gone, who knows where? Now that love is dead.

Dear John (Another)

I'd rather you not visit me, or even make a call.
"It's over", was all she said. Goodbye, and that is all.

It's Final

Nothing you possess, is totally your own.
Even love once shared, is only out on loan.
It's sad, but that's reality, your love, you've both outgrown.
There's little point in going back, now that your love has flown.

Coward

You don't need an explanation, Goodbye, be on your way.
You're just no longer welcome, you are of another day.
I'd rather not explain, so I'll take the wrong way out.
And hope we never meet, on life's long walkabout.

In And Out Of Love

It's letter after letter, when at first you fall.
But at the end, it always seems, a short and sweet phone call.

T.V. Dinners

We would sit there watching telly, with our dinner on a tray.
That could have been my future, so I left without delay.

Relationships

Was there any love left? Or had I just got used to her.
All that I can tell you, is that time passed in a blur.
Should we have parted sooner? The thought, it did occur.
Then she made her decision, it's now, just as you were.

It's That Word Again

From my point of view, you seem gainfully employed.
In that awful bad habit, of cruel Schadenfreude.

Short But Not Sweet

No longer required.
Her love has expired.
Of me, she has tired.
The one she desired.

Faults

Don't suck your fingers, it puts me off.
And raise your hands, when you need to cough.
Nor don't suppress, that weary yawn.
Is it any wonder, that our love is worn.

Stranger

I'm embarrassed to have known you, your standards seem quite low.
I hope you never mention me, to anyone you know.

Bubbles

You were my second love, but certainly not my first.
I loved her. But not like you. You made my bubble burst.

Not Yet!

Redemption may be, not too far away.
But not from my lips, I would like to say.

W, P And G

I'm not quite sure where to put our love under.
W for Worthless, or P for Pointless.
But certainly under G for Gone.

Shall I Send A Card?

Sorry to hear of your sad decline.
But you did deserve it, my ex-Valentine.

Ill-Fitting

Certainly on reflection, we were never really suited.
Your need to be so selfish, it just seemed so deep rooted.

Yes! It Was Me

Remove the pedestal, from where she fell.
Who erected it? I couldn't tell.

Days End

The end of days, it's all one way.
It's what you wanted, I had no say.

Very Soon

There will be a price to pay, you'll see.
Not now, not soon, but eventually.

Perhaps a change of subject
for a while, to 'other things'

Home Is Not The Place I Knew

Home is not the place I knew, where fields
of wild bluebells grew.
Where people knew each others' name,
while growing up seemed one long game.
When ignorance was surely bliss, long
before my first sweet kiss.
A lasting memory of days gone by, that's
my home in my mind's eye.

Innocence had its part to play, in my
perception of yesterday.
When days seemed endless, with sun-kissed
skies, and the elderly were considered wise.
I knew so little, out-lived each day, with few
dark clouds or shades of grey.
The more you know, the less you see, that
life is one long mystery.

Life's corridors are the common ground, that we
journey through to the place
we're bound.
Then childhood is, merely fantasy, as we
head towards what's yet to be.
That longing need of home back then, if I
could, I would, return again.
I see it now, but then I'm caught, in
between lost dreams and thought.

There's little wrong with a backward look,
at the lessons learnt, or the path you took.
To view the world through childlike eyes,
distinguish truth from wanton lies.
Naivety may be the word to use, to
question my distant childhood views.
Of the place I lived, where time went slow,
but time is the thief of life, I know.

True character is built upon, a place
beyond, that is so long gone.
Lay the cloak of doubt across our youth,
then the passing years may cloud the truth.
Who needs to know, against your will, too
much, too soon, where time stood still.
No, home is not the place I knew, how I
miss those days that I wandered through.

The Sea

The sea, the sea, oh! Let it be.

You take out all, without a thought,
You hardly eat all that is caught.
You leave your waste upon its bed,
You hunt all life until it's dead.
You use it for your selfish needs,
You plant your poisoned toxic seeds.
You roam the oceans in your tanker ships,
Causing death and mayhem with your oil slicks.
You behave as if the sea is just,
A place to dump old hulks of rust.
Perhaps too late for your shammed concern,
As the day will dawn, when the tide will turn.

Don't Judge Me

Perhaps even worse than being judged by other people's standards,
Is to be misjudged by those who matter.

Let It Happen

Time and tide, oh let it wait.
Leave life's answers, down to fate.

Live It

Nothing matters in the long term, but I'm certain it matters now.
So live your life, take a risk, unless you've forgotten how.

More Misery Please

Do you realise that the happier you are,
The more you miss out on life?

Life Expectancy (1)

So we expect to live, three score years and ten.
But I want more. Please let me start again.

Life Expectancy (2)

So growing old can be fun, according to the wise.
Am I the only one who thinks, those words are downright lies?

The Others

Of those we feel no need to speak,
Whose character, is cold and weak.
Can we respect the end they seek?
So let them lie, their outlook bleak.

Welcome To The World

An inch to the left, you're surrounded by fame.
While an inch to the right, you're the man with no name.
It's all a result, of life's fickle game.
But I quite like it here, I'm so glad I came.

Be Proud

At least the errors that you make, show that you have lived your life and tried.
Better that, than just sit back, and lose your inner pride.

Who Knows?

There seems a lot of inner anger, when there should be inner peace.
As our morals keep on failing us, will our selfishness increase?

Join The Queue

The religious amongst us, cannot guarantee.
That the place they are heading, will find room for me.
Shall we all form a queue, then wait patiently?
I for one, if I felt, could cry hypocrisy.

Please

Spare us from the T.V. cooks, with their non-stop talk and their series books.
We've had enough, take the hint, together with your herbal mint.

Ageing

Ageing, it happens, at the end of the day.
It's the price for living, not the price that we pay.

Are You In?

Why not follow the crowd? You will feel that you belong.
You can sing it high or loud. Same hymn sheet and same song.

Stand Up And Be Counted

You never think of taking sides,
You're silent, but the truth it hides.
In formed opinions, you see little sense,
As you just sit there, on the fence.

Snow (Day One)

It will never settle, or even last,
It's just a little overcast.
I know it's coming down quite fast,
But it's just the usual arctic blast.

Snow (Day Two)

It came, it settled, the world stood still.
An inch of snow, or at least ten mil.

Who Wanted A White Christmas?

The snow continued falling and then it came again,
By December's end, I hoped and prayed for rain.

It's Here!

It's here, it's global warming,
But the days are bitter cold.
Deep snow and ice is forming,
Excuses? They're on hold.

Calling All Egotists

As wonderful as you think you are, we're getting a little bored.
With your constant waffle about yourself, you shallow, selfish, fraud.

Our Saviour With A Guitar

I've just flown in, to tell you why,
You shouldn't feel the need to fly.
Your carbon footprint, is awfully high,
I must fly off, I know you'll try.

How Soon?

Your numbered days, you won't be missed,
You fading, shallow, egotist.

We Can't Wait!

You will pay for your arrogance, although who knows when?
But we all will be watching. We can't wait until then.

When?

When second rate guys, telling us lies, are running the nation.
All losing the plot, promises forgot, a no-win situation.
But we're all in pursuit of our dreams, with no destination.
Can only end one way it seems, in complete ruination.

Expenses – Your Maker Awaits You

So you did it for the money,
That makes you morally unclean.
We can only hope, you don't lose your seat,
The one downstairs, I mean.

Scoundrels

You're supposed to help us others,
Occasionally you do.
But most of all you spend your time,
In helping yourselves, too.

Gravy Train

I seem the type of person, with an awful lot to give,
I'd like to become a new M.P., where is it that you live?
I could buy a second home, when I eventually gain a seat,
Then can live on my expenses, I'm sure to be discreet.

Awfully Sorry

It's just the kind of error, that anyone could make,
I hope you do not blame me, for my genuine mistake.
I tried to keep it quiet, I'm sorry you found out,
I suppose you'll make me pay, at election time, no doubt.

Squeaky Clean

You can look and keep on looking, but you will find little fault with me.
Didn't anybody mention, I'm an Honourable M.P.
My tracks are quite well covered, as anyone can see.
I'll never resign, from the house, down by the River T.

Help

I'm just a singular voice, with so little choice, out there but needy.
While you bleed me dry, living your lie, looking after the greedy.

To You Apologists

I don't need your apology, you weren't even there.
You were not even born then, so why should you care?
Of course you regret it, but their pain you can't share.
So leave well alone, their hurt, let me bear.

Self Protection

Self praise and self pity, don't let them take hold.
Don't trust them, just treat them, like enemies of old.

Armistice Day

I remember that day, when my heart cried out loud.
I did so much care, of those men, I felt proud.
My sadness and tears, were lost in the crowd.
I thought of their bravery, at once, my head bowed.

Why?

They went, they fought, no questions asked.
While others, in their glory basked.
The truth, just like their fate, was masked.
Never were those questions asked.

Harry Pamplin – Hero – One Of Many

The Great War for Harry, ended the 30th of June.
Disabled on duty, only two years too soon.
A few toes blown off, but got on with his life,
A Honourable discharge, then home to his wife.
The discharge certificate, spelt his name incorrect,
But for Harry and friends, we have tremendous respect.

No Return Home

He rushed everywhere, he wouldn't be late,
He'd be first on the train, he just couldn't wait.
A seat at the front, that suited him fine,
Was he on the right train? He hadn't noticed a sign.

At the next station, others clambered aboard,
There were women and children, onward they poured.
The journey seemed endless, he sensed their great fear,
Weeping young women, was all he could hear.

The crying grew louder, as they journeyed along,
He now felt that something, was seriously wrong.
More people climbed on, when they stopped for a while,
With the carriage now so crowded, with no trace of a smile.

He asked himself why, had he rushed on to the train,
It had all been so pointless, with so little to gain.
Where were they heading, he hadn't a clue,
He felt safe in this country, for he wasn't a Jew.

A short while later, the journey was through,
Then soldiers appeared, there were more than a few.
Down from the carriage, he stepped, with the thought,
What sort of train, had he willingly caught.

Marched across country, the passengers were led,
Weary and hungry, with thoughts left unsaid.
Barbed wire fences, then came into view,
The moment he saw them, he suddenly knew.

The train he had caught, had arrived at a place,
Where people were treated, according to race.
He argued he'd caught, the train by mistake,
An innocent traveller, he cried, for God's sake.

His words were ignored, as he was herded inside,
A large airless building, with no place to hide.
There'd be no return home, he'd committed no crime,
He'd just caught a train, at the wrong place and wrong time.

The following are extracts from love letters received, during four relationships.

They are not published to satisfy any ego, or as a conceited act by the recipient, but to show all the emotions that being in love creates.

To prevent any embarrassment to the writers of the letters, the senders first initial is used at all times.

PART ONE

Letters From 'G'

BRIGHT, THOUGHTFUL AND LOVING.
SHE DESERVED SO MUCH MORE HAPPINESS.

You have started something now. It's been years since I wrote letters and I forgot how compulsive it is, when you get going. You will have to put up with them, and it's all your fault.

I think my writing is getting a bit tired. I shall have to stop. I wanted to write something serious though, so you don't think that I'm a complete idiot.
I've thought of something serious – wait for it. Why are your eyes so dark? I've never seen eyes that dark before. It's quite unnerving.

I'm leaning on a copy of the Pied Piper. There are stacks of mice and rats in it. I'll lend it to you one day, so that you can learn to draw them properly.

I hope you phone me tomorrow, because I'm dying to listen to your telecommunications voice again. I love hearing you talk. Please talk to me lots and lots, not compliments and that stuff. Just conversation talk.

Thanks for all your letters, they were all as smashing as ever. You will have to find me a safe, so that I can lock them away.

By the way, what was all that stuff about talking fish and forests that walked? I don't remember good old days, when things like that happened. I always thought figs really did grow on trees – don't they?

I read your letter at the bus stop, going home tonight. I felt like a schoolgirl. There were stacks of people at the bus stop, and I didn't feel like sharing my precious letter. I kept giggling, which is quite embarrassing when you are on your own, in the middle of a crowd.

Did you get Ben cleaned up alright? (Man's best friend). I hope you didn't get into trouble for getting him dirty. It wasn't your fault, as there were so many puddles to play in. Irresistible, if you are a dog kind of person, like Ben is.

I'm sorry I was so awful today. I can usually steer my way out of such black moods, but you have turned my whole world upside down. Nothing is the same as it was. I locked all my feelings away a long time ago, and you come along and let them all out again, just like that. Check! How could you do that, and so easily?

Sorry if I talked a lot last night, but I reckoned you ought to know me a bit better, before things got out of hand. I'm a very crazy, mixed up nut case, complicated and mad. I also talk too much when I'm nervous, although I do like silences. (Friendly ones, that is).

I've opened up to you, but you are still a closed
book to me. I've only read the summary on the
back cover, and I am greedy to know a lot more
about the real you.
I think you're lovely and I reckon you could be
the best friend I ever had and hope you will
remain so, for the rest of my life.
But right now, it goes further than that.

I don't believe it, pure coincidence. 'How
can I be sure' has just come on the radio.
Beautiful song. I wish you could hear it.

—※—

This letter is going to be serious.
That's how I am feeling right now and you
are to blame for that. I think you implied
that I am a coward, well perhaps I am.
Running scared is what I call it, but I don't
expect you, or anyone else to understand.
That's how it is for me. I'm afraid of liking
people too much, as it hurts.
I used to be a very affectionate, generous,
loyal type of person, but I've had all that
knocked out of me over the years, and like
I've told you before, I'm all bitter and
twisted. You see, people like me have no
defence system, so the only solution, is to
shut down the emotions.
If the guard is there, it is fixed, which
means I am able to cope with most things
calmly and coldly, so I can take a great deal
of verbal and emotional abuse, without too
much effect.

Oh, I wish I could have seen you today, as I reckon we are fated and have been from the start. It's a shame. Do you think we will ever get it together?

Did you really pick up the pieces, after I ripped up the letter, in your car? I hope that there was nothing incriminating, as I never read it. I'm sorry, you will have a lot of trouble putting it together. In fact, it's a bit like me.

You are getting quieter and quieter and I'm getting more and more worried that we are not going to work. I think I love you and I don't want things to go wrong and lose you already.

Do you realise, that it's taken me 40 minutes, to write one page? That's because I'm thinking and not writing, but they are not the sort of things you can put into words. Sort of daydreams really. But if I'm not writing them down, you can be assured, you're in them.

—※—

How I got into this I still don't know, but I'm not giving up, if you can put up with me. I want you, but you don't know how much. Please don't give up on me yet, as it will work out eventually.

I'm sorry I rushed away from you today, as I'm not brave enough. I wanted to kiss you goodbye and show the entire world I don't care what they think, but I'm quite a coward sometimes.

Can I spend dinner time with you again please. When it's convenient for you, because I don't want to disrupt your life completely. (Well I do, but that's just selfish).

I've just heard the most beautiful version of 'Will You Love Me Tomorrow?' Have you ever listened to the words? You should.

To say I love you, without really meaning it, is criminal, and I feel very strongly about words, as you cannot take them back.
I'm truly sorry about staying silent on a very vital point, as I think it means a lot to you.

Please cool down on the 'Honey Talk' as I can't handle much more. You're totally irresistible, and I love you, but I can't cope with it all. I need time to think. Oh God, I've said it now. But I love you and words are so important, as they carry such a crucial message.

What are you doing to me? I don't even know where I am anymore.
I think I love you and I didn't mean to write that.

An hour is not long enough, not when I want
you, as much as I do.

If you wanted me to bring you tea in bed, I
would. As I could spoil you, and if you wanted,
I would stay there and kiss you and love you,
until your tea got all forgotten and cold.

I must get going, as my coffee is getting cold, but
I hope I'll be seeing you soon. (I think that was
a little, nagging doubt). I can't help it, as I still
don't believe what's happened to me. I swore I
would never fall for anyone again (too risky).
But here I am, head-over-heels. I think of you
constantly and in fact, I was thinking of you,
when I woke up this morning.

My darling, sweet, gorgeous, beautiful, sorry.
Thanks, what a smashing day. I really love your
company and I would have walked another
twenty miles, just to stay with you a little longer.
I wanted desperately to touch you, but I didn't
dare, as I can't trust me these days.

I really must stop writing now, or I'll never get
up. I wish you were here, as I love the wee small
hours. They are rather special, it's a lot like the
dawn. Just special, for sharing with someone
special (extra special, if it was you). I don't want
to stop writing, as it's like you are here when I
write to you, but I suppose I must. Sleep well. I
love you.

Can we go and watch the boats and things,
like we did on that Saturday morning,
when all this is over and done with. That
was such a lovely morning. I miss you.

I'm sorry if I keep backing off from you, it's
just that if I allowed myself to respond too
much I wouldn't have any control at all, so
stop tempting me. I don't know if I feel
better when you come to visit me, but it
makes the longing stronger and the
resistance lower. I miss you terribly, and
wish you would write to me to tell me
what you are feeling, and where we go
from here.

I'm so wrapped up in my immediate
problems, that I forgot to ask you. What do
you want from 'us'? Where are we
supposed to be heading? What will
become of us? I need to know how you see
things, from your side.

I still don't believe last night. Did you
mean all of the things you said? I've never
taken much notice of flatterers and line
shooters before, but you shoot the nicest
lines. You seemed sincere, I hope you were.
I'm missing you already.

I want to be with you. I miss you terribly
and it's so much worse, now that I have
actually admitted (not only to you, but to

myself as well – it was a bit of a shock you know) it out loud. I really didn't know. I know that sounds daft, but I don't think I had any idea just how intensely I felt. (Good grief, I'm going to frighten you off. I'm going to change the subject).

I'm beginning to feel very furtive, about our assignations. Gosh! I've just looked up assignation in the dictionary. Guess what it said? Quote: 'Illicit lovers meeting'. Huh! Chance would be a fine thing. God I'm getting very brazen.

Do you realise what I'm going through for you? When I think of some of the suggestive remarks I keep making (I'm blushing), I never used to be so forward. (In fact, I'm getting a bit pushy, you ought to put me down).

Gosh! I want you now. I was tempted to phone you, which would be mad of course, hence this letter.
Small consolation, but I can't help it, as I get high on you. I'm hooked, and I don't care whether you like it or not. I think that you are going to have trouble with me, so watch out. Don't say I didn't warn you.

Somehow, I think for the first time, I'm truly lost for words. What am I to say? I've done it now. I've made the appointment for Saturday 24th April. A momentous occasion.

Thanks for the lovely letter, it was smashing
and I've read it a thousand times already.
You are right about things going very fast,
as I still don't believe what's happened. I
hope that I'm not making a fool of myself,
as I need a lot of reassurance.

Oh, hell!
I'm so scared. I shall be going out in
twenty minutes, but that seems a lifetime
away. When I leave the house, I shall be
about to change my entire life, although I
doubt I have the courage, but I have the
determination. It's scary.
In a very short time, I shall be jumping into
bed with a man I have only been close to
for five days. It's incredible, as I'm not that
sort of girl.
I always was a good girl, but the rules have
changed in the last few years, for nobody
waits anymore.
After all, I saved myself and look what I
saved myself for. Good God, what an idiot
I was, but I hope I'm alright, I'm a little out
of practice, but hope I'm not making a
complete fool of myself.
I've never done anything like this before,
but I hope it means something to you.
Ten minutes to go. I need help. I need you.

—※—

(CATASTROPHE FOLLOWED – But then
that's the way love is).

I shall find it very difficult to face you, later
today, so I felt that I ought to write to you.
It's all feelings again, as words are
inadequate, for the feelings I have churning
around my heart.
Broken hearted isn't a strong enough
description, smashed to smithereens and
squashed into a pulp, would be nearer. I
love you and want you, but I bring you so
much trouble. But the happiness you
brought to me was like the sunshine,
unexpectedly on a rainy day, or like a sweet
breath of air, to a drowning man.

It is possible to make other people happy.
You made me very happy for a while, at a
time when I didn't think that I could ever
be happy again.
Thanks a million. I'll never forget.

I need you, love you and want you very much.
I just thought you ought to know.
It doesn't mean you have to do anything
about it, just try to understand, that I can't
help loving you.

Remember, I put it into words for you
once, long ago.
There is never any of me, left over for me.
Just me myself.
This is very important, as I'm never going
to tie anyone down,
Because I don't ever want to be tied again.
I've had it with that, but that doesn't stop
me loving you.

To You: **The Iceberg – nice guy, but a bit of a heartbreaker.**

With Love: **In Loving Memory.**

From Me: **Miss Gullible** – Clown of the year,
who despite all attempts not to,
she fell for some guy.
Contrary to all resolutions, taken long before
the brief encounter, never to trust anybody ever
again, and inevitably got all hurt
and broken up again.
If she ever believes any more of the stuff people
try to fool her with, she will need to be put away
for a long time, but it's doubtful that she will
ever really lose all her faith in human nature, or
in the gold at the end of the rainbow, or in the
light at the end of the tunnel – well not entirely.
Can she be saved? Who knows? Do you?

We used to have such good conversations. I
think I admired most your ability to see
everything in black and white. So
uncomplicated, he will put me right – put
everything into perspective for me, so I can see
where I'm going – I thought. Having read your
letter, I think that black and white is your one
big failing, as nothing in life is just black and
white. How can I make decisions without
considering others. That to me is impossible, as
it's the way in which we touch each other's lives
as we go along, that makes those lives.

———※———

I'm beginning to feel cheap about the whole
thing, which I never felt that way about it
before. It was all so very special to me. You
brought me out from my brick walls of self
protection, and make me feel again, for the first
time in years.

There is so much I wanted to say, but I'm
making such a mess of it.
You have your own life to lead, your friends and
your sports and things, and a mum who loves
you (I miss my mum very much, these days).
But most of all, you have your life. You're free.
(Master of your own destiny). I seem to have
nothing.

I don't know if I can ever recover from the
insecurity and complete lack of self confidence
that I am left with, as I have nothing left to fight
with.
I feel a bit like an empty shell, and only fear
remains, working its way through every stroke of
my being, as my nerves are shattered and my
spirit is dead.

Were you playing games with me? Taking me
for what you could get. Somehow, I hadn't got
you figured that way. I believed you when you
talked of love and if you remember, it was your
word, long before I allowed myself that luxury.

It's very difficult to write to you, and convey
with any accuracy, the depth of those feelings.
It is also difficult to untangle the great mixture
of different emotions, that are constantly
battling around inside, fighting for attention.
I think it's possible that I have been to the
extremes of most of the human emotions – if
not all – in the last few months.
It hasn't been good for me, as no one could go
through it all and not be affected by it, quite so
drastically.

I wanted to show you why I am a coward. It
isn't something I've just made up. It's been a
slow and painful process.
I wonder how long it will take to undo all the
damage done to my character? As long as I can
keep some of my self respect, I can face anything
that fate throws at me, and I will survive. But I
wish I was free now, while I am
young enough to live.

I don't see you, or talk to you properly anymore.
I hate the way things are and I dread to think
what's going to happen in the not too distant
future.

I miss you. If only I could touch you and hold
you and let you give me the courage,
I lack so badly now.
God, how deeply I feel for you. It hurts all
the time.

No one can take away the hurt. It's almost a year
and the pain is still as sharp as ever. Why can I
not get over it? I still love you. The feeling is so
strong, that it overwhelms me. That's why I run
away, when you get near.

I have felt the need to write to you for a long
time, as you are the only one I can express myself
to, freely. You promised me once that you would
remain my very good friend, no matter what
happened. You know what happened. You
alone, know all of it.

You gave me such happiness. Made me feel so
good. I doubt even you know how much it all
meant to me, or how completely I love you.
It was worth all the days of my life, for just one
moment of loving you.
I love you and miss you, and I don't know what
I'm going to do, for the rest of my life.

I love you and loved you, as you made me so
happy.
I just wanted to write to you one more time.
I think I've just written my Epitaph.
Take care of yourself my darling. I will always
love you.

PART TWO

Letters From 'J'

SWEET, HONEST AND FAITHFUL.
SINCERITY, THAT CAME FROM HER HEART.

I know you think I am too young for you,
but bloody hell, what does it matter how
big the gap. I wouldn't care if you were 96,
let alone 36. I would still feel the same way.

I know you think I am in a hurry and I'm
sorry I give you that impression, but what
we both have is time, and lots of it. I will
wait for however long it takes.

I understand that you don't wish to be tied
down to devoting yourself to one person, as
I know you sometimes meet more than one
woman a night. But I like you for what
you are and the way you live. I would
accept that you want to remain free.

I understand that you think it would be
best if we waited a year or so, but I doubt it
very much if my feelings will change, even
though yours will.

I remember you saying that you would see
me soon. I know I see you five days a week
and I'm grateful for that. But just knowing
you still care for me, means more to me
than making love.
Please be honest. Tell me if you don't care
any longer, or are not interested, because I
want to know where I stand with you.
Because I don't know anymore.

You just don't know me at all. Oh, you
think you do. But you can't. If you think
of some of the things you do. You said to

me today that if you ever went out with me, it wouldn't last. Because I would find someone else within a short time, but how wrong you are.

What I said earlier about 'packing you in', was rubbish. How can you pack someone in, you aren't even going out with.

I have grown much closer, to you, even though I may not show it and that's what hurts. Knowing you could never feel the same for me, as I feel for you. I'm sorry, I guess it's just the way I am.

All I have ever wanted in life, is to love someone so much that it hurts, and them to love me equally in return. Then in a little while, to give birth to a beautiful baby, made with the love we have for each other, and my husband to be there at the birth. I don't think that is too much to ask for, is it?

I have thought very deeply what might happen between us. I feel that you do not really want to go through with this, but you are willing to, as you think it will make me happy and change my outlook on life.

I will meet you wherever is best for you.

P.S. As long as it's not outside my dad's dairy.

I always said I would stay pure until I got married, but that was until I met you. So I don't think you realise how I feel, knowing you never really cared for me.

I'm sorry for the way I have been acting recently, I am disappointed in the fact that I thought we would have been closer after Saturday. But nothing has changed, has it?

So what you really mean is, that making love to me, means absolutely nothing to you. If this is so, I don't think this is worth carrying on with.

I'm not a kid you can give sweets to, to stop me crying. So don't try and sweet talk me round, because I have just had enough, OK?

You know I hate ignoring you, as our friendship means so much to me.
I hope we will be talking to one another very soon, when I have pulled myself together and snapped out of this stupid irritableness, I seem to be surrounded in.

It's funny, but I don't know what I would do without you sometimes, as you always seem to cheer me up, when I am down, and you are always there, when I need you. P.S. I'm sorry!

Thank you for putting up with me
for so long.
You have taught me a lot and
I'm very grateful.

Over the past ten months, you have been
the perfect friend to me. Always willing to
talk when I needed someone to talk to.
The lovely things you would say to me,
putting up with my moods and always
being able to cheer me up, no matter how
down I feel.

The record that I wanted you to listen to on
my tape, sums up what you do for me. You
light up my life.

All the letters you ever sent to me, are here
with me.

I wanted you to come to the flat so much,
so that we could be together, just once. I
know it doesn't really mean anything to
you, but there's nothing on this damn
earth, I have ever wanted so much.

I told you today that I cried last night, but
it wasn't because I wanted to. It was for the
simple reason that I am so glad you are part
of my life.
I do need you.

Have you ever missed someone so much,
that it hurts?
Well that's how much I missed you, the
week I went away.
You were on my mind, from the moment I woke
up, until I went to bed.

I know you still want her, don't tell me you don't.
So I would appreciate very much, if you would
finish our relationship, as I can't do it.

I know you like G. very much, but she is married
with children, and I know that M. was also
married. I just don't want you to be hurt a second
time, as I care what happens to you.

I would like to know if what I overheard, is true? I
have noticed myself that you and A. are getting on
better and better. Perhaps it's her you really want?

You told me never to believe rumours about you.
Now I find that they are true.

I'm sorry for the way I have been treating you over
the past week. I hate myself for it. I don't even
know why I'm taking it out on you, as you haven't
done anything to upset me.

You know I would never finish with you, but you did say that you only want what you can't have, and that doesn't include me. So therefore, if we finish now, it will give you more of a chance to have what you really want, and also to be happy.

I thought that if we stopped speaking to one another for a while, my feelings would die. Unfortunately, there has been no change so far.

I know you don't hurt, but I do, very easily, and today, I'm hurting.

I hope you find real happiness one day, with someone who will treat you better than I have. I'm sorry.

I used to love the lovely things you would say to me. The way you would look at me, and the gentle way you would touch my hair and face. Don't worry about me, as long as we can remain as good friends, I can't ask for more than that.

—※—

Just writing to say sorry for letting you down on Tuesday. I know I should have phoned, as it would have been the decent thing to do, but I didn't have the courage. You have probably guessed why I let you down. Yes, he phoned me, and everything is wonderful, so I couldn't risk losing him by meeting you. I've found something very special, and just don't want to spoil anything.

TWENTY PLUS YEARS LATER, I RECEIVED THE FOLLOWING MEMO, VIA A FORMER WORK COLLEAGUE.

'I have recently found out that a very old and dear friend was working at your office and you keep in touch with him. I used to work with him, over twenty years ago. He is a lovely man and I admired him greatly. When you next speak to him, tell him I was asking about him and hoping he is well and very happy.'

PART THREE

Letters From 'D'

CARING AND HONEST.
PERHAPS A LITTLE IN LOVE, WITH LOVE ITSELF.

I'm sorry that Wednesday evening was such a
disaster, so I have decided to write to you,
because when I'm put on a spot, I like to try and
control my tongue, so that I will not say
anything I might later regret, that could be
subject to recrimination.
I hope you can find it in your heart to forgive
me. Please do not misconstrue any of this as an
act of tenacity. I do hope we can go out again,
whenever you want, in any capacity, and have an
enjoyable time. Next week if you like, you could
let me know.
In spite of everything you say and do, I cannot
help but love you, with all my heart.
In the meantime, I'll carry on trying to win the
lottery, so that you can marry me for my money.

Anything really worth having involves risk, but
there is no risk with me, you've backed a winner.
I need you, desire you and desperately want you.
Please let go, emotionally.
You know exactly what's in my heart and what I
feel for you.

To my sweetheart. Come back to me my darling.
I need you so very much. I love you for always
and forever.

Darling, please listen to me. I want you to be
fair to me, because I love you more than ever.

To my darling. Please love me always and forever, as I
do you. Be true and faithful in every way,
as I am to you.
A day never passes when I don't think of you, so
please be there for me, as you have in recent times,

and cherish what you have every day, as I cherish
you. Never let it go, no matter what.
I need you my true love, more than ever, so don't
push me out on the side line. Thank you for
being there for me, in troubled times. I love you.

Darling. You mean more than anything else in the
world to me, and I love you, with a love that will
never die. You are completely special to me in every
way and I need you desperately. All my love forever.

I've missed you more than ever this week sweetheart.
How much I've longed for your touch, and your
gentle caress.
As the weeks go by, I grow more and more in love
with you and I want to love you for all time and ever.
I love you truly with all my heart and I always will. I
love your gentleness and tenderness, and you never
shout at me, when I say, or do, the wrong thing. I
love to please you darling, and need you, like the
flowers need the rain.
My bed is so empty, and I'm so lonely without you. I
feel safe and content in your arms and in love. I hope
so much that you long for me, as I do you.

By the time you will read this, I'll be in bed, no
doubt, lying awake, thinking of you.
The thought of you and the joy you have given
me are inexpressible, but one thing I know for
sure, is that my first waking thought will be of
you my darling, and you will remain in my heart
both tomorrow and the beginning of a new day,
until we can be together again. What we share is
precious, beyond comparison.
It is a true gift and a true love, to be treasured
and cherished, for all time.
Keep me in your heart. Goodnight
and God bless.

You are the best thing that's ever happened to me and every day, I love you, more and more. How can a love that's completely wonderful, keep growing?
Because we were made for each other, and meant to love one another. You are my true love.

My darling, I'm so happy when I think of you. It's a privilege to love, and a joy to be with you. Love you, for always and forever.

My darling is my true and only love. Mine, mine, mine.

Darling, you mean everything in the world to me. I love you with all my heart, nobody could ever replace you.

May the Lord be gracious unto you, and give you peace in your mind and joy in your heart.

You are so special, and I need you so much. Please love me always.

—————————

PART FOUR

Letters From 'M'

MY FIRST LOVE (THE ONE)
THE LETTERS WERE WRITTEN OVER
A PERIOD OF SIXTEEN YEARS

Early 1980's

I've been wondering lately, if you would mind us
having a chat. A chat about nothing really, but I
would just like to see you again.
If you don't ring, I will understand. Nice talking to
you again.

Please call your Pen Pal / Friend.
Do you realise that we love each other so much already,
and we are not even lovers.
Can't wait to see you tomorrow and always remember,
that I love you more than you will ever know.

This silly letter isn't sent for any reason, other than I
want you to know I love you and always will love you,
until the day I die.
I know we will be together (that's if you are still
single and you feel the same).
I have discovered that I can't live without you.
P.S. Thank you for everything.
Doesn't that sound awful. It isn't meant to sound like
that. I mean, thank you for loving me and making
me very happy and making me fall in love for the
first time in my life. Thank you, for you.

I love you, I hope you are not sad. As you say to me
so often, we must not be sad, we haven't got time.

I love you. I feel terribly sad today, so I'm not going
to write much. I just love you and never want to be
without you.
I want to go home to you tonight and I want to sleep
with you, and I want to make love to you.

I miss you so very much, as I love you, and love everything about you.
I cannot live without you anymore, and I just hope that you keep on loving me. I don't think you will, but a short time of us being together, is better than nothing at all.

I'd rather be with you than anything in the world, but I know that tomorrow, I will feel unsure all over again. It's quite amazing. I thought I loved you all I could, and then we made love, and I love you so much more, and every time I see you, I love you more.

I was empty until I met you. I knew there was something missing, but I thought it was me, never satisfied. I wasn't in love, just stable, as stability was what I needed then.
I love you so much and just curl up thinking about you for a while, and I feel so beautiful, if we have made love.

Well anyway, I'm going to the loo and to change the bed. I love you, I want you, I need you, I adore you, you are so beautiful when I am with you. I am so happy even sitting in your car, when you're not there. It's your car, I love it. I love you.

P.S. When we are together,
can we have a baby soon, please?

Do I love you? I didn't imagine that
love was like this.
Do you realise that I will love you all your life?
I would love you to have a son. Our son. That I
could give you and make you happy.
I've never felt like this before and saying all that has
made me feel happier. I feel closer to you.

I've been hoping that I was pregnant this month, but
today I have been having tummy pains, so I don't
think I am. Do you worry that I will become
pregnant? Do you really want me to be? I do,
because I would just love to have your child, and I
don't, because I don't think I would make a
good mother.
We might drift away and you would get fed up of me
and nappies and leave us.
But then again, I would rather have you for a while,
than not at all.

I hope that your cold is better, somebody tells me
that you're cracking up! Are you? That's nice. I've
never had that effect on anyone before.

Why do you love me? Do you think I'm pretty? I'm
not now, but if you had seen me when I was 19 years
old, I was beautiful, even if I say so myself. But I've
changed a lot and I'm fuddy duddy.

Shall I come to you early tomorrow at 7.30am and
sleep for a while?
Can I? But I won't, as I will be too shy to do that, but
God, how I want to.

I just want to thank you for loving me and I promise, well partly promise, not to eat garlic or smoke again.

I hope that you had a nice game of cricket tonight and that you caught somebody out again. Next time, I will watch it all the time. Although I did yesterday, but sometimes I was lighting a cigarette. (Smoking has a lot to answer for, hasn't it?)

You're beautiful. I keep picturing you talking and laughing when you are making love to me, and it fills me up.
I love you so much, it's so stupid. I cry when I'm sad and cry when I'm happy.

I have just read all your letters and I do love you so much. Nobody in the world makes me feel like you do. At times, frequently now, I think I know that you are falling out of love with me.
Yes it's my fault, but it's tragic.

I've just called you, and I'm going to call you again, and I have got butterflies. I can spell really, honestly I can. It's just one of the million effects you have on me.
P.S. I want to ask you, if you're not too busy, because you might be doing something else. If you would (but only if you can), want to (because you can say no and I won't mind). If you could possibly meet me for lunch tomorrow, (or today, as you are reading this letter).
Can you let me know as soon as you can, so that I can sort out how I am going to feel.

I know that you are very irritable tonight for some
reason (probably me). I don't see how I can make
you happy, I really don't. I've been dying to see you
all day, because I upset you last night, but looking at
you now, I wonder if you came here for me, or the cat.
If I shrivelled up, you wouldn't notice, would you?
Please say something to me now – no, you are
looking at the cat – never mind – I love you so much.
Can we have a dog at Christmas,
that nobody else wants, please.
I know you've come here to see the cat,
as I'm boring, aren't I?
Heidi (cat) is more important than me. I love you all
the world.

You tell me to tell you things, well you hurt me today.
One whole day gone, and we didn't tell each other
that we loved each other. So I know you don't want
me today.

I'm writing you a letter, in case you don't
want to see me anymore.
I'm dying to see you, always am, I love you so much.
I hope that you're not in a bad mood today.
It's funny, that sounds horrible when I say that, but
you are not, you are wonderful.
I've been on the Sun bed today and my face is
looking awful, but I've bought some new make-up to
hide it. You should still like me.

Monday morning and I'm going mad, as I can't sleep,
or stop thinking about you.
I'm hurting so much, because I make you sad too.
I love you.

Anyway, going now, and if I can find some Valium, I'll
see you in Heaven (only joking).
I love you and I always will. You've made me much
happier than I ever thought I could be, as making
love with you is the most beautiful thing in the
world. (Apart from you telling me that you love me
and that you would never leave me – and you
laughing and winking at me).
You will never get this letter, so I can say what I like.
It will only make you sad and I want you to be happy.
I want to make you happy. I want to be with you
forever, and have your children. I want you.

When we are together and even married one day,
with children and dogs, and you wanted to go, you
could quite easily, as I don't expect anything, not even
your love, forever. Although, will I say this in twenty
years time, I don't know?

What are you doing now? You must be dancing with
someone, or you will be soon. I wonder if you will kiss
her and hold her tight and want her. Will you? Because
I will dream and think about you, doing that all night.
I'm sick of being sad, as I love you so much, but these
words are so ordinary. I wish you could feel, what I feel
for you. I was watching you tonight in the car and
you're so beautiful. I wanted to put my arms around
you and hug you. My wants are so simple, a little house,
you and a baby.
Then I would be completely happy. Maybe I want a
baby for the wrong reasons – most of all, I want a baby
for you. I want to see you play with them and read
stories at night to them and to kiss and love them. I
want that so much, I'm sure we would make beautiful
children, born out of such unbelievable love.

I'm writing you this because I feel OK today and I want to make you happy, because I know that you have been worried about me. What was her name on Sunday, and why did you stay until 2.30? You do love me as much as you used to, don't you? You can tell me if you don't. I will understand, honestly. I won't cry or anything, as I'll just leave you alone and you will feel better then. So please tell me.
Don't keep doing horrible things, hoping that I will go away, because I love you so much, I won't. I don't want to hurt anymore. I do think you love me, because you wouldn't make love to me if you didn't, would you?

Couldn't you have rang me from the club? No you couldn't, could you, it's not your style, is it? You didn't ring me when you went to a club with all your friends before Christmas, and I sat up half the night. You big horrible slimey toad, and that is meant in the horriblist possible way.

Jealousy – I have never felt this before, as no man has ever done this to me. It frightens me, especially what you told me about Scorpios.
The thought of you out with someone else is so hurtful, so if you are going to play around, tell me, and I will go. You know I love you, but I don't think you love me.

—※—

The strange thing is, well you know I love you, but when you are not with me, or talking to me, I don't feel that you care. You see, basically, I'm very immature. You are so much more grown up than me about things, that you seem to handle everything really well.

I will probably never call you again, because I feel so
sad and because I want you to chase me a little.
I really shouldn't be telling you my reasons, should I?

It's now 1.30 and you haven't called and I don't
suppose you will. I'm so mad with you.
I fall in love with you and I need you,
but you don't care.

Sometimes, you make me feel bloody unwanted.
From the minute I woke up this morning, I felt so
happy, then what happens, you are playing squash.
It isn't that I mind you playing squash, I couldn't
anyway, but it's the way you say, 'I would rather be
seeing you', and that's it, as I am crying on the other
end of the phone. How can you do it? I don't
honestly think you can possibly realise how much I
love, need and want you. You don't, do you?

I'm frightened to say anything to you now, because
you will say something horrible and hurt me again.
This can't continue, can it?
Today, I know you don't love me, last night I think
you hated me, when I needed you
more than ever before.
I love you and if you believed that (which I know you
don't), you would know that we will be together.

I wish you wouldn't let me walk off, when I'm upset,
you do it every time. One day I'll walk off and we
will row. I love you.

You sound as if you don't give a damn about me.
Well if you want us to part, tell me, don't do it like
this. I love you more than I thought I could love
anybody, but I would rather you say.
I cannot cope with being hurt, by the man I love.

I'm missing you so much. I can't, we can't, carry on
like this anymore. I'm so frightened.
It's the hurt, it's so horrible, I wish you wouldn't feel
it, but I feel pretty awful now and I need you.
Do you know I have never needed anyone, never in
my life, and I need you.
I can't see any way out of this, at all. Never mind, eh!
I love you and I want you, but I'm frightened, because
I know I would never ever leave you and that would
be wrong for us.
I would crack up and so would you, I think.

I have read that letter several times and you don't, or
didn't think that I loved you at all.
Your attitude, it's ridiculous, and if you don't want
me, go, and if I know you have been with other girls,
I will die, so it's up to you.
Silly stupid me, thought I had met someone who
was different.
I've even eaten for you today and have only had
eleven cigarettes and I wanted to tell you I loved you
and everything would be OK.
Well, this is the last time I wait for a call from you,
ever. I haven't acted like this ever and I'm not going
to start now, when you don't even care.

—※—

I can't love anyone else physically or mentally.
I need you and I'm going to be with you forever.
You will probably hurt me one day, but it's
worth the risk.

I hope you weren't sad last night, because I was, I
missed you, as it seemed ages since I last saw you, yet
it's only been one day.
My friend feels that I ought to go away for a while
and think. I don't want to think. I just want you. I
love you so very much – I honestly do.

I have read your letter so many times. I want to call
you and want to see you, but the thing that is
upsetting me, is that you don't think I love you.
I love you more than anything in the world, but I'm
so frightened of doing things wrong, and ruining us.
Are you interested in these letters anymore?
Or are you fed up with them?
As I was thinking today, there are so many things you
used to do and don't do anymore. I suppose that's
natural really, because you are used to me,
but it's a shame really.
I will always love you and we will
never part – you are all my life.

I hope you are OK. I haven't hurt you have I?
I feel awful.
Anyway, it's all over now, isn't it? Please don't be sad, I
will love you forever, and hope I will see you one day.

P.S. Please buy the Phil Collins album.

Late 1980's / Early 1990's

Take care of your leg. I love you so much, I hate it. Actually, a few years ago, I saw a film with Meryl Streep and Robert De Niro, called 'Falling in Love'. Watch it sometime.
It reminded me of us at the time, it certainly does now.

I can't see you today, but I miss you terribly when I don't see you.
I probably even feel more for you, and think of you all the time.
You are so beautiful and I still get butterflies, every time I see you.

I know you're in control, as I tried really hard last week and it sort of worked, but not anymore. I wish I was hard and then I wouldn't care, but I don't like being like that, because it is frightening.
I wish I had never rung you up, as I want us to make love all the time, but I'm scared and then I feel silly. After all, I'm 28 now and shouldn't be so immature. Anyway, my beautiful man, I love you dearly and desperately want us to be together.

We mustn't love each other – well only secretly. It's got to stop, we can't, won't, mustn't, spend Sunday together, because it will finish me off. I'm not just saying it for fun either. So please, please, be strong and don't let anything happen. A friend told me that you only pretend to like me, so that you can get your own back and I shouldn't take you seriously. (But I don't believe it really). We will both get hurt, because it's not meant to be, but it's nice to know we love each other. I love you dearly.

Hope you are fine – one of my friends mentioned to me that fine stands for:- Fed-up, insecure, neurotic and emotional. I hope you are only emotional. I miss you and have missed you all day. Some days are worse than others. I wish it didn't hurt so much. I know you used to say that, it was good to hurt, but I've never thought so. I love you and it's 4.45pm – please call me.

I love you when you laugh and smile. I love you when you are serious and trying to be tough. I love you when you leave notes on my car, and ring me, and tell me I'm too intense, and laugh at me. I love you for so many things. I'll always love you and always have, although I didn't realise it was so strong before.
Thank you for never giving up on me. Even though we may not be together, remember, I'll always love you. I always have and always will.

I love you ever so much and miss you all the time. Right now, I would like to be on an island, just us, wouldn't that be Heaven?
I have dreamt about you a lot recently, and I don't like that, because we are always very close in my dreams, but when I wake up, you are never around. Perhaps one day that will change – I will always hope so.
I wish we were together, as I would just love one night with you and wake up together. I think that would keep me going all year.
I love you, in case you didn't know.

I presume that you are playing another game of squash. I can't blame you really, as it's all hassle, isn't it?

I've waited to see you smile at me (then I would know everything is OK) for ages. I'll go now, but where are you?

Have you decided without make-up I'm not too nice, or have you had enough?

So sorry about Ben (man's best friend). I don't know what to say, because I know you loved him so much. Miss you lots.

I haven't sent you a nice card because it's just not a good idea.

Happy Christmas.

I'm sorry I feel like this, as it hurts a lot today, but I will probably feel better tomorrow. I love you so much and I'm so frightened. It can't be a casual game to me, as I want you all the time you see. I really think this has got to stop – I can't concentrate – work is suffering. I want to see you. I'm sorry I feel like this.

Just a note to say I love you, and please can we go to Fridays, on Thursday evening? – You would like it.

Have a nice evening, although I wish it was with me, as I love you so much and always think of you, when I wake in the night.

I wish we could turn back the clock seven years – it's a long time isn't it?

It's a good job that I love you, as I waited from
6.15 to 6.55.
If I take Vitamin C, will you be on time?
Hope you had a good game of squash – sorry I
couldn't wait, but I'm dying for the loo. All my
love as always.

I love you – even though you think I'm a pain in
the ass.

Dearest darling. I love you and still think about
you all the time.
I hope your spot is better.
My whole body aches for you (corny but true).
I've never had that before, except from you.
Not good!

Every time I think of you this morning, I either
get the giggles, or my tummy keeps on flipping.
I keep getting goose bumps when I think of you,
and am very much in love with you today. I feel
so happy, you've certainly got to me today. I
haven't felt like this before – it's great.

You do want me don't you? Sometimes I don't
think you do at all, and I cannot cope with this
anymore.
Today I wish I was miles away, alone, but if I was
alone, I would only be missing and thinking
about you.
Why did I fall in love with you? I'm glad I did,
because you are beautiful and I love you.

Early, Mid And Late 1990's

THE LETTERS CONTINUE, FOLLOWING HER MOVING
TO THE NORTHERN HIGHLANDS OF SCOTLAND

I was just thinking. If we were never to see each other again, and only ever wrote – when we die, what will be made of our letters, or our life together. Deep, isn't it?

I love you and I wish I could be with you all the time, to watch you play cricket and be part of your world. I can't, and I hate it.

Thank you very much for the beautiful card and even more beautiful words. It made me sadder than normal.

An hour has passed since I wrote to you and I can't remember what I was trying to say, except that I am a better person and it's just as well we split up then, because we may have done, at a later date. It might have upset us, more than it did then. You were never really gutted like I would have been, if you had left me, were you?

I love you and miss you lots, and think of you and our past all the time. I want you so very much, it hurts.

I received your letter today and it was lovely. I don't think you should play so much sport, especially with your bad leg (broken), but I can't stop you, can I? It's just as well we are not married, because I wouldn't let you play so much. Yes, I would love to marry you, but you are probably only asking because you know I can't. I will send you a photo of my cat Henry. He was wild and abandoned, and I love him to death. Have you anyone now? Are you interested in anyone? Do you sleep with anyone? I make love with you in my dreams.

Hope you are OK. I'm dying to read your letters and see your photos.
I do love you, but it's all too late, I think – no it's not really – we will just be old and wrinkled, but at least we will be happy.
Why, oh why, did we split? My fault, I know. I hate myself for it.

I'm quite worried actually, because I'm feeling clingy now, and I haven't felt like this since our early (and later, come to that) days.

I wish we could have a short time together, but
once I had that, I would want more. I wonder if
you know how much I regret leaving you. I
regretted it before I did it, but I was so
frightened and confused, as I just wanted to get
away from all the heartache.
Why didn't someone tell me that I would be
miserable and regret it.
Thank you for still loving me and wanting me. I
adore you and wish you were not alone.
I wish you had a beautiful wife, and lots of
children, and dogs, and cats. You deserve it.
Unfortunately, all I can provide is the cat. I'm so
pleased you like Henry.

I love you. You know that don't you? I have
always loved you.
I never stopped loving you, even when you
thought I did.
If only we had been somewhere else that night,
we would have stayed together forever.
I know it.
That's why I contacted you in the first place.
Didn't you ever think of that? I've always
wondered about that night, surely you knew
how much I wanted you?

I sat in the car after the funeral and read all your
letters and cards again.
I can't begin to explain how they make me feel.
Incredibly sad, really hurting heart sad, but they
also make me feel happy, and make me want to
be with you, so much. It really hurts. What is to
become of us?

—✳—

I'm thinking about you all the time this week
and miss you so much, which does absolutely
nothing for my stress levels. I explained to my
friend that we have never made love since we
finished, although I love you the most, and the
reason for that I think, is because, I love you so
much. I have always felt very special with you,
as sex was beautiful, and not just lust.
I always felt shy and unsure of what to do, and
my heart could just break when I think of it.
She thinks that we are in a very sad situation,
and that part of my stress is
self denial and longing.
She feels that we should spend time with each
other and work it out, and get on with our lives.
Nobody will ever love me as you did, which I
realise now.
My shrink thinks that I am regressing, as I feel I
cannot get over you.
I don't really want to. That's another part of the
problem.

It's such a lovely day, and these type of days
remind me of Sutton Park. The beautiful walks
and the absolutely gorgeous clinches.
Looking back, the happiest days of my life are
the ones I spent with you. I had 3 or 4 days and
nights with you, and I took Ben (man's best
friend) to the park, then cooked you a meal.
I sunbathed all day in your mother's back
garden, then waited for you to come home. I
was so happy then. I love you my darling.

I am sitting by the River (Ness), having a cigarette, as it's a beautiful day and most of the tourists have gone home. I do wish you wouldn't keep telling me nice things, because they just make me worse, and you have no idea how much I would love to run away with you. I need you so much.

I wish with all my heart that I could re-live my life again. I get very annoyed with people who have regrets, but I do wish with all my heart, that I was with you, now. I think about you often, especially since I have been ill, I need you, I think that's what it is. But c'est la vie.

Please don't worry that it's Thursday and you haven't called me yet. Your letter was so beautiful, but don't think you can get around me, because you can't. I could have missed you lots, and been dying to hear from you by now. Anyway, don't worry about me, I'll just go out with Alistair tonight instead. He is just waiting to fall in love with me. I love you all the world, and it's all your fault.

What was the Sutton Park Hotel like, last night? Did you have a wonderful time? Did you fall in love with someone else? What time did you get home? Were you alone? Lie to me if necessary. Do you remember New Year's Eve at the Beehive? The pub where I smashed the car!!! Sorry. I love you and think about you all the time. I even dream about you all the time, but am I going to dream forever? Eventually you will find someone else and fall in love, properly.

Are you sure that you still want me? Seriously,
are you? Because life would be a lot different for
you – but I can take it if you can – can you?
You must be sure, for how do you know you still
want me sexually and it's no good thinking you
do, but how do you know you do? Please tell
me you want me.

Thank you my beautiful man for the
photograph of you and the wonderful letter. Yes,
of course I will marry you. I am married to you
really, because I have never been able to get over
you and whenever I think of love, romance and
happiness, I always thought of you.

I want to talk to you all the time, and it's agony
for me when I have to leave you. I'm going into
Inverness at lunch time today – can you please
meet me for lunch?
Do you remember when I used to make you
meet me at Rackhams, for coffee, at lunch times?
How you hated it. I do love you. I hope you are
not lonely. I wouldn't be upset if you met
someone else – honestly I wouldn't. As long as
you are happy, I'm happy, but just don't love her
as much as you love me, but love her enough to
make yourself happy. Enjoy yourself – but not
too much. All my love, forever.

Really, if I'm truthful, I wish you would find
someone you could love. I really wouldn't mind,
as I'm not in a position to mind. At least you
wouldn't be lonely, as someone would be there
when you get home, from squash, football and
cricket. Someone who absolutely adored you,

and wouldn't mind your hobbies. The more I write this, the more I think it's a stupid idea, and I think I would die if you fell in love, and didn't love me anymore. I'm a really selfish person, vain and selfish, a bit like you really. Not that I dislike you for it. I love the fact that you don't need me, as much as I need you. It's probably what keeps my interest.

Reading this letter back, it's such a lot of twaddle. It's just as well that you know me.

I am so amazed that you won't let me run away, as it would be the answer to all my prayers, and you won't let me. Stupid for us to talk about it really, but it's probably because you don't want to give up squash or cricket, or something like that. I absolutely love you so much, it hurts, and I'm sorry that I was so grumpy today, but it's only because you are so stupid. It's not my style to face people, when I can run away, is it? I love you to death and would love a holiday with you, but it would spoil me for the rest of my life, especially if I couldn't run away with you. That was bitchy, but I do love and adore you, but I can't see us getting together, so that's why I'm sad.

When you said yesterday that I must not run away and must take things slowly, is that because you are not sure? I can understand it, as you have not seen me for ages, and I have probably changed, and am not as young anymore. If you are unsure and would like to make it less intense, I would like it if you told me so, then I can change. My friend said I would probably never return home if I saw you, but I said that I would, as you wouldn't let me run away. I was hoping you would change your mind. I would have done. I love you.

I am talking to you while I am writing, and really miss you, and wish you felt happy. I have always thought that you would make a wonderful father, but we could always adopt. Although once we had each other, the pain of it would eventually go away, and we would be happy together. I love you so much, it's agony. You wouldn't understand how much I miss you and think about you.

—❋—

Have you fallen in love with anyone else yet? I hate to think of you with someone else, close to them. It's quite hurtful.
If you found someone to go out with occasionally, who enjoys sport and animals, I would be happy for you. I think, as long as you didn't love her. All the things I say to you, I have never said to anyone else, as I have never felt with anyone else, the way I feel with you, and about you. Thinking of you, still gives me butterflies in my tummy.
Nothing has been as deep or beautiful, as with you, which is sad really, because, here I am, writing about it and not experiencing it, which I should have been all this time.
P.S. When we are married, I can still have facials, can't I?

I have just rang you and a woman answered the phone, and I said that I had rang the wrong number. I know I have written many lines saying that I could accept you having a relationship, but I am so shocked. It's unbelievable. Who is she? I have just rang you again and you answered. You sounded beautiful and I love you.

I absolutely adore you and dream and think
about you all the time, which my friend tells me,
is unhealthy. I have always loved you, and I wish
you had known that, even when we finished.
I cried for weeks, because I missed you, and it
took me ages to contact you, because I thought
you would hate me. I know I had spoilt the way
that you could love me. Always remember, just
how much I love you and think about you, even
if you are sleeping with somebody else.

My heart is hurting today, more than normal.
It's because I have spoken to you, probably. I do
love you, and only want to be with you. When
will I? I don't care if we don't get married, as
long as we are together. Is that OK? I love and
miss you so much. The whole thing is so futile.
What on earth are we doing?

I wish I could make you happy, but I just love
making you angry. I used to love making you
mad with me, because you were so cute, when
you were in a tantrum. It's funny the things I
remember, but you getting mad with me, I do
remember. Perhaps because it was
a frequent occasion.
Your anger and everyone else's anger were always
totally different. Your anger was calling me a
'pain in the ass', telling me to grow up, and
saying how irresponsible I was, then being
wonderful to me.

—※—

On Christmas Eve, I went with my mother to
Midnight Mass. It was beautiful, I haven't been
for years. I cried buckets at church and told God

how much I love you. I don't really think we will be together. Why should I be that happy? We will carry on writing and calling until I am free, and then, when I am, you will be so scared that you will stop speaking to me altogether. I know that will happen. And I don't care that I shouldn't start a sentence with **And**, and I don't care that I make hundreds of spelling mistakes. And I love you so much, perhaps it's just as well.

Hello sweetheart.
I love you and miss you and so much want to be part of your life. I wish I could moan at you for always playing squash and coming home late. I wish I could.
A psychoanalyst I know, thinks I talk about you and think of you all the time, to punish myself, for what I did, and (you'll like this), because you are my true love and I know I can't have you and probably never will. I cried buckets at that and have been very sad since. I miss you and wish we could make love and make a beautiful baby. I so much wished that I could be pregnant by you. We tried so hard really, didn't we? The times I would be sure I was pregnant, after we made love. I love you all the world.

My dearest darling. I feel so guilty that I could cry. It doesn't mean that I don't love you and miss you and still think about you all the time, as you have no idea how much I need you. But not at the cost of something awful happening, as we wouldn't like each other very much.
I have always lived in Walt Disney's world, I think. Love from Henry (cat), too.

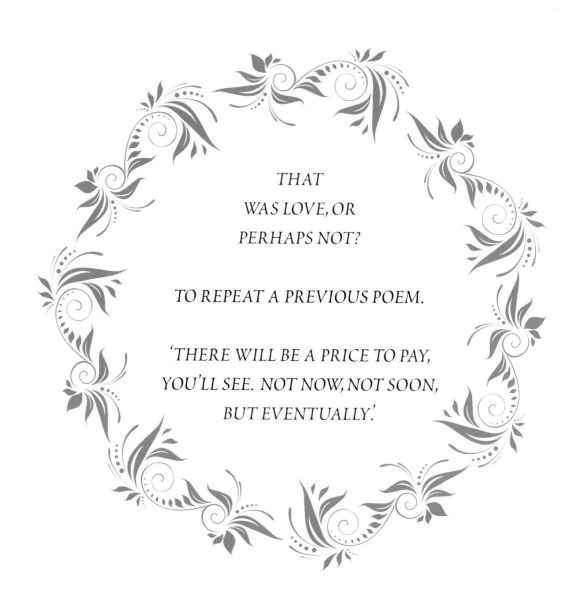

THAT
WAS LOVE, OR
PERHAPS NOT?

TO REPEAT A PREVIOUS POEM.

'THERE WILL BE A PRICE TO PAY,
YOU'LL SEE. NOT NOW, NOT SOON,
BUT EVENTUALLY.'